This Planner belongs to:

&

_____
first and last name

_____
first and last name

_____
wedding date and location

2023

January

S	M	T	W	T	F	S
1	2	3	4	5	6	7
8	9	10	11	12	13	14
15	16	17	18	19	20	21
22	23	24	25	26	27	28
29	30	31				

February

S	M	T	W	T	F	S
			1	2	3	4
5	6	7	8	9	10	11
12	13	14	15	16	17	18
19	20	21	22	23	24	25
26	27	28				

March

S	M	T	W	T	F	S
			1	2	3	4
5	6	7	8	9	10	11
12	13	14	15	16	17	18
19	20	21	22	23	24	25
26	27	28	29	30	31	

April

S	M	T	W	T	F	S
						1
2	3	4	5	6	7	8
9	10	11	12	13	14	15
16	17	18	19	20	21	22
23	24	25	26	27	28	29
30						

May

S	M	T	W	T	F	S
	1	2	3	4	5	6
7	8	9	10	11	12	13
14	15	16	17	18	19	20
21	22	23	24	25	26	27
28	29	30	31			

June

S	M	T	W	T	F	S
				1	2	3
4	5	6	7	8	9	10
11	12	13	14	15	16	17
18	19	20	21	22	23	24
25	26	27	28	29	30	

July

S	M	T	W	T	F	S
						1
2	3	4	5	6	7	8
9	10	11	12	13	14	15
16	17	18	19	20	21	22
23	24	25	26	27	28	29
30	31					

August

S	M	T	W	T	F	S
		1	2	3	4	5
6	7	8	9	10	11	12
13	14	15	16	17	18	19
20	21	22	23	24	25	26
27	28	29	30	31		

September

S	M	T	W	T	F	S
					1	2
3	4	5	6	7	8	9
10	11	12	13	14	15	16
17	18	19	20	21	22	23
24	25	26	27	28	29	30

October

S	M	T	W	T	F	S
1	2	3	4	5	6	7
8	9	10	11	12	13	14
15	16	17	18	19	20	21
22	23	24	25	26	27	28
29	30	31				

November

S	M	T	W	T	F	S
			1	2	3	4
5	6	7	8	9	10	11
12	13	14	15	16	17	18
19	20	21	22	23	24	25
26	27	28	29	30		

December

S	M	T	W	T	F	S
					1	2
3	4	5	6	7	8	9
10	11	12	13	14	15	16
17	18	19	20	21	22	23
24	25	26	27	28	29	30
31						

A

2024

January

S	M	T	W	T	F	S
	1	2	3	4	5	6
7	8	9	10	11	12	13
14	15	16	17	18	19	20
21	22	23	24	25	26	27
28	29	30	31			

February

S	M	T	W	T	F	S
				1	2	3
4	5	6	7	8	9	10
11	12	13	14	15	16	17
18	19	20	21	22	23	24
25	26	27	28	29		

March

S	M	T	W	T	F	S
					1	2
3	4	5	6	7	8	9
10	11	12	13	14	15	16
17	18	19	20	21	22	23
24	25	26	27	28	29	30
31						

April

S	M	T	W	T	F	S
	1	2	3	4	5	6
7	8	9	10	11	12	13
14	15	16	17	18	19	20
21	22	23	24	25	26	27
28	29	30				

May

S	M	T	W	T	F	S
			1	2	3	4
5	6	7	8	9	10	11
12	13	14	15	16	17	18
19	20	21	22	23	24	25
26	27	28	29	30	31	

June

S	M	T	W	T	F	S
						1
2	3	4	5	6	7	8
9	10	11	12	13	14	15
16	17	18	19	20	21	22
23	24	25	26	27	28	29
30						

July

S	M	T	W	T	F	S
	1	2	3	4	5	6
7	8	9	10	11	12	13
14	15	16	17	18	19	20
21	22	23	24	25	26	27
28	29	30	31			

August

S	M	T	W	T	F	S
				1	2	3
4	5	6	7	8	9	10
11	12	13	14	15	16	17
18	19	20	21	22	23	24
25	26	27	28	29	30	31

September

S	M	T	W	T	F	S
1	2	3	4	5	6	7
8	9	10	11	12	13	14
15	16	17	18	19	20	21
22	23	24	25	26	27	28
29	30					

October

S	M	T	W	T	F	S
		1	2	3	4	5
6	7	8	9	10	11	12
13	14	15	16	17	18	19
20	21	22	23	24	25	26
27	28	29	30	31		

November

S	M	T	W	T	F	S
					1	2
3	4	5	6	7	8	9
10	11	12	13	14	15	16
17	18	19	20	21	22	23
24	25	26	27	28	29	30

December

S	M	T	W	T	F	S
1	2	3	4	5	6	7
8	9	10	11	12	13	14
15	16	17	18	19	20	21
22	23	24	25	26	27	28
29	30	31				

2025

January

S	M	T	W	T	F	S
			1	2	3	4
5	6	7	8	9	10	11
12	13	14	15	16	17	18
19	20	21	22	23	24	25
26	27	28	29	30	31	

Febuary

S	M	T	W	T	F	S
						1
2	3	4	5	6	7	8
9	10	11	12	13	14	15
16	17	18	19	20	21	22
23	24	25	26	27	28	

March

S	M	T	W	T	F	S
						1
2	3	4	5	6	7	8
9	10	11	12	13	14	15
16	17	18	19	20	21	22
23	24	25	26	27	28	29
30	31					

April

S	M	T	W	T	F	S
		1	2	3	4	5
6	7	8	9	10	11	12
13	14	15	16	17	18	19
20	21	22	23	24	25	26
27	28	29	30			

May

S	M	T	W	T	F	S
				1	2	3
4	5	6	7	8	9	10
11	12	13	14	15	16	17
18	19	20	21	22	23	24
25	26	27	28	29	30	31

June

S	M	T	W	T	F	S
1	2	3	4	5	6	7
8	9	10	11	12	13	14
15	16	17	18	19	20	21
22	23	24	25	26	27	28
29	30					

July

S	M	T	W	T	F	S
		1	2	3	4	5
6	7	8	9	10	11	12
13	14	15	16	17	18	19
20	21	22	23	24	25	26
27	28	29	30	31		

August

S	M	T	W	T	F	S
					1	2
3	4	5	6	7	8	9
10	11	12	13	14	15	16
17	18	19	20	21	22	23
24	25	26	27	28	29	30
31						

September

S	M	T	W	T	F	S
	1	2	3	4	5	6
7	8	9	10	11	12	13
14	15	16	17	18	19	20
21	22	23	24	25	26	27
28	29	30				

October

S	M	T	W	T	F	S
			1	2	3	4
5	6	7	8	9	10	11
12	13	14	15	16	17	18
19	20	21	22	23	24	25
26	27	28	29	30	31	

November

S	M	T	W	T	F	S
						1
2	3	4	5	6	7	8
9	10	11	12	13	14	15
16	17	18	19	20	21	22
23	24	25	26	27	28	29
30						

December

S	M	T	W	T	F	S
	1	2	3	4	5	6
7	8	9	10	11	12	13
14	15	16	17	18	19	20
21	22	23	24	25	26	27
28	29	30	31			

C

Table of Contents

Ideas/Research Wedding Themes

Wedding Theme Idea & Color Scheme #1

Wedding Theme Idea & Color Scheme #2

Wedding Theme Idea & Color Scheme #3

Ideas/Research Gifts

Gift Ideas For The Maid/Matron Of Honor & Best Man

Gift Ideas For The Bridesmaids

Gift Ideas For The Groomsmen

Ideas/Research Music

Intro Song for Grandparents and Parents: _____

Artist: _____

Grandparents of Bride: _____
Grandparents of Groom: _____
Parents of Bride: _____
Parents of Groom: _____

Intro Song for the Bridal Party: _____

Artist: _____

Bridesmaid   Groomsmen

_____   Escorted By: _____
_____   Escorted By: _____
_____   Escorted By: _____
_____   Escorted By: _____
_____   Escorted By: _____
_____   Escorted By: _____
_____   Escorted By: _____
_____   Escorted By: _____
_____   Escorted By: _____

Flower Girl(s)   Ring Bearer:

_____   _____

_____   _____

Maid of Honor   Best Maid:

_____   _____

Notes:

_____
_____
_____
_____
_____

Ideas/Research Music

Intro Song for Bride and Groom: Artist:

_____   _____

Bride and Groom Introduced As: _____

Bride and Grooms First Dance: Artist:

_____   _____

Whole or Half: _____   Bridal Party Joins In: YES   NO

Blessing By: _____

Toast by Maid of Honor: _____

Toast by Best Man: _____

Toast by Other: _____

☐ Anniversary Dance / Song: _____
                                        Artist: _____

☐ Centerpiece Giveaway: _____
                                        Artist: _____

☐ Cake Cutting Song: _____
                                        Artist: _____

☐ Bouquet Toss: _____
                                        Artist: _____

☐ Garter Off: _____
                                        Artist: _____

☐ Garter Toss: _____
                                        Artist: _____

☐ Garter On Bouquet Winner: _____
                                        Artist: _____

☐ Bride's Dance With Father: _____
                                        Artist: _____

☐ Groom's Dance With Mother: _____
                                        Artist: _____

☐ Last Song For Bride & Groom: _____
                                        Artist: _____

Preferred Songs

☆☆☆☆☆ Song: _____ Artist: _____

☆☆☆☆☆ Song: _____ Artist: _____

☆☆☆☆☆ Song: _____ Artist: _____

☆☆☆☆☆ Song: _____ Artist: _____

☆☆☆☆☆ Song: _____ Artist: _____

☆☆☆☆☆ Song: _____ Artist: _____

☆☆☆☆☆ Song: _____ Artist: _____

☆☆☆☆☆ Song: _____ Artist: _____

☆☆☆☆☆ Song: _____ Artist: _____

☆☆☆☆☆ Song: _____ Artist: _____

☆☆☆☆☆ Song: _____ Artist: _____

☆☆☆☆☆ Song: _____ Artist: _____

☆☆☆☆☆ Song: _____ Artist: _____

☆☆☆☆☆ Song: _____ Artist: _____

☆☆☆☆☆ Song: _____ Artist: _____

☆☆☆☆☆ Song: _____ Artist: _____

☆☆☆☆☆ Song: _____ Artist: _____

☆☆☆☆☆ Song: _____ Artist: _____

☆☆☆☆☆ Song: _____ Artist: _____

☆☆☆☆☆ Song: _____ Artist: _____

☆☆☆☆☆ Song: _____ Artist: _____

☆☆☆☆☆ Song: _____ Artist: _____

☆☆☆☆☆ Song: _____ Artist: _____

☆☆☆☆☆ Song: _____ Artist: _____

☆☆☆☆☆ Song: _____ Artist: _____

☆☆☆☆☆ Song: _____ Artist: _____

☆☆☆☆☆ Song: _____ Artist: _____

☆☆☆☆☆ Song: _____ Artist: _____

☆☆☆☆☆ Song: _____ Artist: _____

☆☆☆☆☆ Song: _____ Artist: _____

☆☆☆☆☆ Song: _____ Artist: _____

☆☆☆☆☆ Song: _____ Artist: _____

☆☆☆☆☆ Song: _____ Artist: _____

Thoughts & Ideas

Thoughts & Ideas

Thoughts & Ideas

12 Months Before

- ○ Announce your engagement
- ○ Define your total budget.
- ○ Select a date for your wedding.
- ○ Start putting together a guest list.
- ○ Research ceremony and reception venues.
- ○ Think about what kind of wedding.
- ○ Pick a location for your wedding.
- ○ Throw an engagement party.
- ○ Hire a wedding coordinator.
- ○ Book a wedding planner.
- ○ Research and book rehearsal dinner, ceremony and reception venues.

THINGS TO REMEMBER:

9 to 12 Months Before

- ○ Select your wedding party.
- ○ Searching for the wedding dress.
- ○ Start thinking flower girl dresses.
- ○ Book DJ for ceremony and reception.
- ○ Book a photographer
- ○ Interview and select an officiant.
- ○ Start thinking about honeymoon plans.

- ○ Choose a color palette and style.
- ○ Start thinking about bridesmaids.
- ○ Book musicians
- ○ Book a caterer.
- ○ Book a videographer.
- ○ Take your engagement photos.

THINGS TO REMEMBER:

6 to 9 Months Before

○ Order your wedding dress.

○ Finalize your guest lists.

○ Book a florist or select a flower vendor.

○ Book your honeymoon accommodation&flight.

○ Create a registry for wedding gifts.

○ Finalize your ceremony order with officiant.

○ Order your save the dates and mail them out 6 months in advance
   for local weddings, and 8 months for destination weddings.

○ Order your bridesmaids' dresses.

○ Gather mailing addresses.

○ Pick out your cake.

○ Book rooms for guests

○ Reserve any site rentals.

THINGS TO REMEMBER:

3 to 5 Months Before

- O Mail out invitations.
- O Reserve the attire.
- O Arrange transportation for the wedding day.
- O Organize legal documents needed
- O Order your wedding bands.
- O Order wedding favors for guests.
- O Send a guest list to the hosts of your parties.
- O Order other stationery items.
- O Shop for the wedding accessories.
- O Book a hair and makeup trial.
- O Finalize the menu and drink.
- O Schedule beauty appointments.
- O Finalize the order of your reception..

THINGS TO REMEMBER:

2 Months Before

○ Enjoy your bridal shower this month.

○ Double-check with venues and vendors.

○ Purchase a special gift for wedding party.

○ .Begin seating plan and order place cards.

○ Print any signage for your wedding day.

○ Meet with the photographer and videographer to discuss shots.

○ Follow up your guest list.

○ Confirm with your florist.

○ Get your marriage license.

○ .Have your final dress fitting.

○ Write and practice your vows.

THINGS TO REMEMBER:

1 Month Before

- ○ Update caterer with final guest count.
- ○ Pick-up wedding dress & bridesmaid dresses.
- ○ Confirm delivery details with all vendors.
- ○ Bachelor and bachelorette parties.
- ○ Have final meeting with officiant, photographer and videographer.

- ○ Pick-up your wedding rings.
- ○ Pack an emergency kit.
- ○ Confirm honeymoon bookings.
- ○ Assign wedding week.

THINGS TO REMEMBER:

1 Week Ahead

○ Write out the day-of timeline.

○ Have a wedding rehearsal.

○ Have a relaxing massage.

○ Deliver decorations and items to the reception venue.

○ Pack for your honeymoon.

○ Have a manicure and pedicure.

○ Try to get a full night of sleep.

THINGS TO REMEMBER:

On The Wedding Day

○ Check the latest weather forecast.

○ Pack the luggage.

○ Give your marriage license to the officiant.

○ Get hair, makeup etc. done.

○ Give the groomsmen and bridesmaids thank you gifts.

○ Relax and enjoy your wedding day!

THINGS TO REMEMBER:

After Wedding Day

○ Write thank you cards.

○ Make sure all vendors have been paid in full.

○ Order wedding photo prints.

○ Share your wedding photos and videos.

○ Arrange name changes, such as drivers license, passport, bank accounts, insurance, employer and social media!

THINGS TO REMEMBER:

To Do List

TASK	DUE
○	
○	
○	
○	
○	
○	
○	
○	
○	
○	
○	
○	
○	
○	
○	
○	
○	
○	
○	
○	
○	
○	
○	
○	
○	
○	
○	
○	
○	

To Do List

TASK	DUE
○	
○	
○	
○	
○	
○	
○	
○	
○	
○	
○	
○	
○	
○	
○	
○	
○	
○	
○	
○	
○	
○	
○	
○	
○	
○	
○	
○	

To Do List

TASK	DUE
○	
○	
○	
○	
○	
○	
○	
○	
○	
○	
○	
○	
○	
○	
○	
○	
○	
○	
○	
○	
○	
○	
○	
○	
○	
○	
○	
○	
○	
○	

Sample Schedule

TIME	DESCRIPTION
	Wake-up call bride
	Wake-up call groom
	Groomsmen drop off misc items at venue
	Bridal party arrives
	Bride hair and makeup
	Photographer arrives
	Videographer arrives
	Bridesmaids' arrive hair and makeup
	Groom and groomsmen arrive
	Lunch
	Groom & groomsmen change into tuxedos or suits
	Coordinator arrives
	Flowers arrive before photos are taken
	Coordinators set up guest book, favors, centerpieces
	Quick rehearsal with officiant
	Bride gets dressed and touches up makeup
	Family arrives
	Photographer takes detail photos
	Photography session
	Last minute preps
	CEREMONY
	Musicians / DJ arrives
	Music begins 30 minutes before ceremony
	Guests start to arrive
	Ushers start seating guests 30 min prior to ceremony
	Ushers stop seating guests 5 min prior to processional
	Ushers to seat latecomers in isle seats
	Officiant takes their place
	Prelude (welcoming) music begins
	Wedding party lines up for processional
	Attendants proceed down the aisle
	Special guests are seated
	Groom and best man take their place
	Processional (formal entrance) music begins

Sample Schedule

TIME	DESCRIPTION
	Processional starts
	Bride walks down the aisle
	Ceremony begins
	You may kiss the bride!
	Recessional (formal exit) music begins
	Guests move to cocktail hour
	RECEPTION
	Cocktail hour for guests before bride and groom arrive
	Photos with bridal party
	Guests are directed to their seats
	Arrive at the reception
	Bride and groom Grand entrance
	Bride and groom are seated
	Dinner starts
	Best man toast
	Maid of honor toast
	Groom and bride speech
	Cake cutting
	Garter toss
	Bouquet toss
	Sideshow
	First dance
	Father and daughter dance / mother and son dance
	Guests dance
	End of the reception
	Break down and clean up
	Arrive at hotel

Schedule

TIME	DESCRIPTION

Schedule

TIME	DESCRIPTION

Thoughts & Ideas

Wedding Budget Planner

ITEM	BUDGET	ESTIMATE	SPENT
CEREMONY & RECEPTION			
Ceremony location			
Officiant			
Marriage license			
Reception venue			
Catering			
Bar			
Rentals			
Music			
Wedding cake			
Bartenders			
Photo booth			
Transportation couple & guests			
Parking			
Tips and coat check			
Ring pillow			
Flower girl basket			
Guest book			
FLOWERS & DECOR			
Bride's bouquet			
Maid's bouquets			
Corsages			
Boutonnières			
Throw away bouquet			
Flower girls' flowers			
Altarpiece			
Other ceremony arrangements			
Reception centerpieces			
Other decor			
PHOTO & VIDEO			
Engagement shoot			
Photographer			
Wedding album			
Parents' albums			

Wedding Budget Planner

ITEM	BUDGET	ESTIMATE	SPENT
Additional prints			
Videography			
STATIONERY			
Save the dates			
Invitations			
Programs			
Place cards/menus			
Thank you cards			
Other signage			
Postage			
GIFTS			
Attendants (favors)			
Maid of honor			
Bridesmaids			
Best man			
Groomsmen			
Parents of bride			
Parents of groom			
Readers / other participants			
Welcome Gifts			
ATTIRE			
Wedding dress			
Headpiece and veil			
Bridal shoes			
Lingerie/hosiery/ garter			
Jewelry and accessories			
Hair and makeup			
Dress preservation			
Beauty appointments			
Wedding rings			
Groom's tuxedo or suit			
Groom's shoes			
Groom's accessories			

Wedding Budget Planner

ITEM	BUDGET	ESTIMATE	SPENT
Outfit for ring bearer and usher			
Bridesmaids'dresses			
Bridesmaids'shoes			
Bridesmaids'accessories			
Dresses for flower girl(s)			
Children's outfits			
Honeymoon clothes			
OTHER EVENTS			
Engagement party			
Bridal shower			
Bachelorette party			
Bachelor party			
Rehearsal dinner			
Unexpected costs			
HONEYMOON			
Airfares			
Accommodation			
Transportation			
Activities			
Meals and drinks			
Shopping allowance			
Passport and visa			
Vaccinations and medications			
Luggage			
Clothing			
Personal care			
Pet care			
Other			

Wedding Budget Planner

ITEM	BUDGET	ESTIMATE	SPENT

Budget — Purchases

DATE	ITEM	QTY.	COST	NOTES

Vendor – Wedding Coordinator

COORDINATOR NAME:

ADDRESS:

PHONE:

EMAIL:

ITEM	BUDGET	ESTIMATE	SPENT
TOTAL			

NOTES:

Vendor – Wedding Venue

VENUE NAME:

CONTACT:

ADDRESS:

PHONE:

EMAIL:

WEDDING DATE:

VENUE OPENING TIME:

VENUE CLOSING TIME:

ITEM	BUDGET	ESTIMATE	SPENT
TOTAL			

NOTES:

Vendor – Photography

VENDOR:

CONTACT:

ENGAGEMENT SHOOT DATE/TIME:

NUMBER OF PHOTOGRAPHERS:

PHOTOGRAPHER HOURS AT WEDDING:

OPTIONS FOR ADDITIONAL HOURS:

WILL I GET DIGITAL FILES:

DATE THAT FILES WILL BE AVAILABLE:

TURN AROUND TIME FOR PROOFS/ALBUMS:

BACK-UP PLAN IF PHOTOGRAPHER IS SICK:

PAYMENTPOLICY:

CANCELLATIONPOLICY:

ITEM	BUDGET	ESTIMATE	SPENT
TOTAL			

NOTES:

Vendor – Videography

NAME:

CONTACT:

NUMBER OF VIDEOGRAPHERS:

NUMBER OF HOURS AT WEDDING:

OPTIONS FOR ADDITIONAL HOURS:

TURNAROUND TIME VIDEO:

ONLINE HOSTING OPTIONS:

HOW MANY DVDS WILL I RECEIVE:

BACK UP PLAN IF VIDEOGRAPHER IS SICK:

PAYMENT POLICY:

CANCELLATION POLICY:

ITEM	BUDGET	ESTIMATE	SPENT

NOTES:

Vendor – Food

VENDOR NAME:

CONTACT:

PICK-UP OR DELIVERY TIME:

SPECIAL REQUEST:

ITEM	BUDGET	ESTIMATE	SPENT
TOTAL			

NOTES:

Vendor – Drinks

VENDOR NAME:

CONTACT:

PICK-UP OR DELIVERY TIME:

SPECIAL REQUEST:

ITEM	BUDGET	ESTIMATE	SPENT
TOTAL			

NOTES:

Vendor – Stationery

VENDOR NAME:

CONTACT:

ITEM	BUDGET	ESTIMATE	SPENT
TOTAL			

NOTES:

Vendor – Officiant

OFFICIANT NAME:

ADDRESS:

PHONE:

EMAIL:

ITEM	BUDGET	ESTIMATE	SPENT
TOTAL			

NOTES:

Vendor – Attire (Bride)

WEDDING DRESS SUPPLIER NAME:

CONTACT:

FITTING APPOINTMENT 1:

FITTING APPOINTMENT 2:

FITTING APPOINTMENT 3:

PICK-UP DATE:

VEIL SUPPLIER NAME:

CONTACT:

SHOES SUPPLIER NAME:

CONTACT:

JEWELRY SUPPLIER NAME:

CONTACT:

HOSIERY / LINGERIE SUPPLIER NAME:

CONTACT:

ITEM	BUDGET	ESTIMATE	SPENT
TOTAL			

NOTES:

Vendor – Attire (Groom)

TUXEDO / SUITE SUPPLIER NAME:

CONTACT:

FITTING APPOINTMENT 1:

FITTING APPOINTMENT 2:

PICK-UP DATE:

SHOES SUPPLIER NAME:

CONTACT:

ITEM	BUDGET	ESTIMATE	SPENT
TOTAL			

NOTES:

Vendor — Attire (Bridesmaids)

DRESS SUPPLIER NAME:
CONTACT:
FITTING APPOINTMENT 1:
FITTING APPOINTMENT 2:
PICK-UP DATE:
SHOES SUPPLIER NAME:
CONTACT:

ITEM	BUDGET	ESTIMATE	SPENT
TOTAL			

NOTES:

Vendor – Attire (Groomsmen)

TUXEDO / SUITE SUPPLIER NAME:

CONTACT:

FITTING APPOINTMENT 1:

FITTING APPOINTMENT 2:

PICK-UP DATE:

SHOES SUPPLIER NAME:

CONTACT:

ITEM	BUDGET	ESTIMATE	SPENT
TOTAL			

NOTES:

Vendor – Attire (Other)

FLOWER GIRL(S) DRESS SUPPLIER NAME:

CONTACT:

PICK-UP DATE:

RING BEARER(S) TUXEDO OR SUIT SUPPLIER NAME:

CONTACT:

PICK-UP DATE:

USHER(S) TUXEDO OR SUIT SUPPLIER NAME:

CONTACT:

PICK-UP DATE:

ITEM	BUDGET	ESTIMATE	SPENT
TOTAL			

NOTES:

Vendor — Rings

VENDOR NAME:

CONTACT:

BRIDE RING SIZE:

GROOM RING SIZE:

SPECIAL REQUESTS:

PICK-UP DATE:

ITEM	BUDGET	ESTIMATE	SPENT
TOTAL			

NOTES:

Vendor – Music

VENDOR NAME:

CONTACT:

ARRIVAL TIME:

SPECIAL SET-UP REQUESTS:

ITEM	BUDGET	ESTIMATE	SPENT
TOTAL			

NOTES:

Vendor – Favors

VENDOR NAME:

CONTACT:

PICK-UP OR DELIVERY TIME:

ITEM	BUDGET	ESTIMATE	SPENT
TOTAL			

NOTES:

Vendor – Flowers

VENDOR NAME:

CONTACT:

PICK-UP OR DELIVERY TIME:

ITEM	BUDGET	ESTIMATE	SPENT
TOTAL			

Vendor – Decor Rental

VENDOR NAME:

CONTACT:

PICK-UP OR DELIVERY TIME:

ITEM	BUDGET	ESTIMATE	SPENT
TOTAL			

Vendor – Hair

VENDOR NAME:

CONTACT:

TRIAL RUN APPOINTMENT DATE/TIME:

WEDDING DAY APPOINTMENT DATE/TIME:

ITEM	BUDGET	ESTIMATE	SPENT
TOTAL			

NOTES:

Vendor – Makeup

VENDOR NAME:

CONTACT:

TRIAL RUN APPOINTMENT DATE/TIME:

WEDDING DAY APPOINTMENT DATE/TIME:

ITEM	BUDGET	ESTIMATE	SPENT
TOTAL			

NOTES:

Vendor – Cake

VENDOR NAME:

CONTACT:

PICK-UP OR DELIVERY TIME:

SPECIAL REQUEST:

ITEM	BUDGET	ESTIMATE	SPENT
TOTAL			

NOTES:

Vendor – Transportation

VENDOR NAME:
CONTACT:
PICK-UP TIME:
PICK-UP ADDRESS:
DROP-OFF ADDRESS:
PICK-UP TIME:
PICK-UP ADDRESS:
DROP-OFF ADDRESS:

ITEM	BUDGET	ESTIMATE	SPENT
TOTAL			

NOTES:

Vendor

VENDOR NAME:

CONTACT:

PICK-UP OR DELIVERY TIME:

SPECIAL REQUEST:

ITEM	BUDGET	ESTIMATE	SPENT
TOTAL			

NOTES:

Vendor

VENDOR NAME:

CONTACT:

PICK-UP OR DELIVERY TIME:

SPECIAL REQUEST:

ITEM	BUDGET	ESTIMATE	SPENT
TOTAL			

NOTES:

Vendor

VENDOR NAME:

CONTACT:

PICK-UP OR DELIVERY TIME:

SPECIAL REQUEST:

ITEM	BUDGET	ESTIMATE	SPENT
TOTAL			

NOTES:

Ushers

Usher name:

Phone:

Email:

Size:

Usher name:

Phone:

Email:

Size:

Usher name:

Phone:

Email:

Size:

Usher name:

Phone:

Email:

Size:

Usher name:

Phone:

Email:

Size:

Usher name:

Phone:

Email:

Size:

Usher name:

Phone:

Email:

Size:

Notes:

Maid Of Honor & Bridesmaids

Maid of honor name:

Phone:

Email:

Dress size:

Bridesmaid name:

Phone:

Email:

Dress size:

Bridesmaid name:

Phone:

Email:

Dress size:

Bridesmaid name:

Phone:

Email:

Dress size:

Bridesmaid name:

Phone:

Email:

Dress size:

Bridesmaid name:

Phone:

Email:

Dress size:

Bridesmaid name:

Phone:

Email:

Dress size:

Notes:

Best Man & Groomsmen

Best man name:

Phone:

Email:

Suit size:

Groomsman name:

Phone:

Email:

Suit size:

Groomsman name:

Phone:

Email:

Suit size:

Groomsman name:

Phone:

Email:

Suit size:

Groomsman name:

Phone:

Email:

Suit size:

Groomsman name:

Phone:

Email:

Suit size:

Groomsman name:

Phone:

Email:

Suit size:

Notes:

Flower Girl

Flower girl name:

Phone:

Email:

Dress size:

Flower girl name:

Phone:

Email:

Dress size:

Flower girl name:

Phone:

Email:

Dress size:

Flower girl name:

Phone:

Email:

Dress size:

Notes:

Ring Bearer

Ring bearer name:
Phone:
Email:
Suit size:
Ring bearer name:
Phone:
Email:
Suit size:
Ring bearer name:
Phone:
Email:
Suit size:
Ring bearer name:
Phone:
Email:
Suit size:

Notes:

Planning – Rehearsal Dinner

LOCATION:

DATE:

TIME:

FOOD/CATERER NAME:

CONTACT:

ITEM	BUDGET	ESTIMATE	SPENT
TOTAL			

NOTES:

Rehearsal Dinner Guest List

FAMILY/NAME	# OF SEATS	INVITE SENT	RSVP

Planning — Engagement Party

LOCATION:

HOST:

DATE:

TIME:

FOOD/CATERER NAME:

CONTACT:

ITEM	BUDGET	ESTIMATE	SPENT
TOTAL			

NOTES:

Engagement Party Guest List

FAMILY/NAME	# OF SEATS	INVITE SENT	RSVP

Planning — Bachelor Party

LOCATION:

HOST:

DATE:

TIME:

FOOD/DRINKS:

NAME:

CONTACT:

GAMES:

FAVORS:

ITEM	BUDGET	ESTIMATE	SPENT
TOTAL			

NOTES:

Bachelor Party Guest List

NAME	INVITE SENT	RSVP

Planning — Bachelorette Party

LOCATION:

HOST:

DATE:

TIME:

FOOD/DRINKS:

NAME:

CONTACT:

GAMES:

FAVORS:

ITEM	BUDGET	ESTIMATE	SPENT
TOTAL			

NOTES:

Bachelorette Party Guest List

NAME	INVITE SENT	RSVP

Planning – Bridal Shower

LOCATION:

HOST:

DATE:

TIME:

FOOD/DRINKS:

NAME:

CONTACT:

GAMES:

FAVORS:

ITEM	BUDGET	ESTIMATE	SPENT
TOTAL			

NOTES:

Bridal Shower Guest List

NAME	INVITE SENT	RSVP

Honeymoon Planning Guide

6 MONTHS OR MORE AHEAD
- ○ Pick your travel dates
- ○ Set a budget
- ○ Research and choose your destination
- ○ Price out airfare, accommodation, transportation and excursions
- ○ Make reservations
- ○ Buy travel insurance

3-6 MONTHS OR MORE AHEAD
- ○ Book excursions and shows
- ○ International travelers, apply for a passport, if necessary, visas
- ○ Get vaccinations if required

1-3 MONTHS AHEAD
- ○ Review your packing list and see what special items need to be purchased
- ○ Purchase luggage
- ○ Find out airline's luggage limits
- ○ Make house-sitting and pet-sitting arrangements
- ○ Purchase a travel guidebook

1 MONTH AHEAD
- ○ Finalize honeymoon plans
- ○ Finalize transportation
- ○ Confirm reservations
- ○ Put together a packing list

1-2 WEEKS AHEAD
- ○ Make copies of your passports, visas, credit cards, traveler checks, license and airline tickets
- ○ Take one copy with you and leave one copy at home with someone reliable
- ○ Write down important phone numbers
- ○ Secure your tickets
- ○ Get some local currency
- ○ Pack what you can ahead of time

1-2 DAYS AHEAD
- ○ Pack a carry-on bag for your travels
- ○ Check the local weather forecast

Honeymoon

Location:
Date:
Average temperature:
High season:
Hotels/resorts:
Pricing:

NOTES:

Honeymoon Travel Details

FLIGHTS
Date:

Departure time:

From:

Airline:

Date:

Departure time:

From:

Airline:

Date:

Departure time:

From:

Airline:

ACCOMMODATIONS
Hotel/lodging name:

Address:

Check-in date:

Check-out date:

Balance at check-in: $

Hotel / lodging name:

Address:

Check-in date:

Check-out date:

Balance at check in: $

TRANSPORTATION
Car rental company:

Pick-up date and time:

Pick-up location:

Drop-off date and time:

Drop-off location:

OTHER

Honeymoon Itinerary

DATE	TIME	ACTIVITY

Honeymoon Packing List

Wedding Vows

NOTES:

Day-Of Kit For The Groom

ESSENTIALS

○ Wedding rings
○ Wedding license and pen
○ Cell phone and charger
○ Driver's license and credit cards
○ Cash for tips and miscellaneous payments
○ Payment envelopes for vendors
○ Groom's wedding vows
○ Groom's wedding thank you speech

ATTIRE

○ Extra pair of dress socks
○ Extra shirt buttons and thread
○ Extra pair of cufflinks
○ Extra pair of shoe laces
○ White handkerchief
○ Lint brush
○ Sewing kit
○ Shoe polish kit

MEDICAL & PERSONAL

○ Pain reliever
○ Hair styling tools, hairspray, hair gel
○ Allergy medication
○ Prescription drugs
○ Band-Aids
○ Breath mints
○ Toothbrush, toothpaste and floss
○ Deodorant
○ Insect repellent
○ Contact lenses, solutions and eye drops
○ Glasses
○ Cologne
○ Shaving kit/mustache or beard trimmer
○ Tissues

MISCELLANEOUS

○ Bottled water & small snack
○ Umbrella or raincoat
○ Emergency phone numbers
   (groomsmen & vendors)

Day-Of Kit For The Bride

ESSENTIALS
- ○ Cell phone and charger
- ○ Credit card or cash
- ○ Bride's wedding vows
- ○ Bride's wedding speech

BEAUTY
- ○ Hair brush, hair spray, comb, and curling iron
- ○ Hair gel/mousse
- ○ Hair styling tools
- ○ Bobby pins and other hair accessories
- ○ Nail polish and nail polish remover
- ○ Nail file and nail clippers
- ○ Tweezers

MAKEUP
- ○ Dusting powder
- ○ Makeup and tools
- ○ Makeup remover
- ○ Small face towels
- ○ Tissues

ATTIRE
- ○ Extra pair of hose
- ○ Buttons
- ○ Safety pins
- ○ Iron and towel, pressing cloth, or steamer
- ○ Stain or spot remover
- ○ Slippers and shoe horn
- ○ Super glue for broken heels
- ○ Alternative shoes for reception
- ○ Earring backs
- ○ Lint brush

SEWING KIT
- ○ Needles, pins, thimble, and scissors
- ○ Thread for gowns and dresses
- ○ Double-stick tape

MEDICAL AND PERSONAL
- ○ Prescription medications/allergy medication
- ○ Pain reliever
- ○ Tampons and pads
- ○ Moist towelettes
- ○ Band-Aids
- ○ Antiseptic and clear bandages
- ○ Hand lotion
- ○ Breath mints
- ○ Toothbrush, toothpaste, floss, toothpicks
- ○ Soap and hand sanitizer
- ○ Deodorant
- ○ Perfume
- ○ Contact lenses, solutions and eye drops
- ○ Glasses
- ○ Tissues

MISCELLANEOUS
- ○ Bottled water and straws
- ○ Snacks
- ○ Emergency phone numbers
  (bridal party & vendors)

Day-Of Kit For The Groom

Day-Of Kit For The Bride

Wedding Guest List

Name	Address	Phone	Invited	Gift Received	Thank you card sent
				○	○
				○	○
				○	○
				○	○
				○	○
				○	○
				○	○
				○	○
				○	○
				○	○
				○	○
				○	○
				○	○
				○	○
				○	○
				○	○
				○	○
				○	○
				○	○
				○	○

Wedding Guest List

Name	Address	Phone	Invited	Gift Received	Thank you card sent
				○	○
				○	○
				○	○
				○	○
				○	○
				○	○
				○	○
				○	○
				○	○
				○	○
				○	○
				○	○
				○	○
				○	○
				○	○
				○	○
				○	○
				○	○
				○	○
				○	○
				○	○

Wedding Guest List

Name	Address	Phone	Invited	Gift Received	Thank you card sent
				◯	◯
				◯	◯
				◯	◯
				◯	◯
				◯	◯
				◯	◯
				◯	◯
				◯	◯
				◯	◯
				◯	◯
				◯	◯
				◯	◯
				◯	◯
				◯	◯
				◯	◯
				◯	◯
				◯	◯
				◯	◯
				◯	◯
				◯	◯

Wedding Guest List

Name	Address	Phone	Invited	Gift Received	Thank you card sent
				◯	◯
				◯	◯
				◯	◯
				◯	◯
				◯	◯
				◯	◯
				◯	◯
				◯	◯
				◯	◯
				◯	◯
				◯	◯
				◯	◯
				◯	◯
				◯	◯
				◯	◯
				◯	◯
				◯	◯
				◯	◯
				◯	◯
				◯	◯
				◯	◯

Wedding Guest List

Name	Address	Phone	Invited	Gift Received	Thank you card sent
				◯	◯
				◯	◯
				◯	◯
				◯	◯
				◯	◯
				◯	◯
				◯	◯
				◯	◯
				◯	◯
				◯	◯
				◯	◯
				◯	◯
				◯	◯
				◯	◯
				◯	◯
				◯	◯
				◯	◯
				◯	◯
				◯	◯

Wedding Guest List

Name	Address	Phone	Invited	Gift Received	Thank you card sent
				◯	◯
				◯	◯
				◯	◯
				◯	◯
				◯	◯
				◯	◯
				◯	◯
				◯	◯
				◯	◯
				◯	◯
				◯	◯
				◯	◯
				◯	◯
				◯	◯
				◯	◯
				◯	◯
				◯	◯
				◯	◯
				◯	◯
				◯	◯
				◯	◯

Wedding Guest List

Name	Address	Phone	Invited	Gift Received	Thank you card sent
				◯	◯
				◯	◯
				◯	◯
				◯	◯
				◯	◯
				◯	◯
				◯	◯
				◯	◯
				◯	◯
				◯	◯
				◯	◯
				◯	◯
				◯	◯
				◯	◯
				◯	◯
				◯	◯
				◯	◯
				◯	◯
				◯	◯

Wedding Guest List

Name	Address	Phone	Invited	Gift Received	Thank you card sent
				◯	◯
				◯	◯
				◯	◯
				◯	◯
				◯	◯
				◯	◯
				◯	◯
				◯	◯
				◯	◯
				◯	◯
				◯	◯
				◯	◯
				◯	◯
				◯	◯
				◯	◯
				◯	◯
				◯	◯
				◯	◯
				◯	◯
				◯	◯

Wedding Guest List

Name	Address	Phone	Invited	Gift Received	Thank you card sent
				○	○
				○	○
				○	○
				○	○
				○	○
				○	○
				○	○
				○	○
				○	○
				○	○
				○	○
				○	○
				○	○
				○	○
				○	○
				○	○
				○	○
				○	○
				○	○
				○	○

Wedding Guest List

Name	Address	Phone	Invited	Gift Received	Thank you card sent
				○	○
				○	○
				○	○
				○	○
				○	○
				○	○
				○	○
				○	○
				○	○
				○	○
				○	○
				○	○
				○	○
				○	○
				○	○
				○	○
				○	○
				○	○
				○	○
				○	○
				○	○

Wedding Guest List

Name	Address	Phone	Invited	Gift Received	Thank you card sent
				○	○
				○	○
				○	○
				○	○
				○	○
				○	○
				○	○
				○	○
				○	○
				○	○
				○	○
				○	○
				○	○
				○	○
				○	○
				○	○
				○	○
				○	○
				○	○

Wedding Guest List

Name	Address	Phone	Invited	Gift Received	Thank you card sent
				○	○
				○	○
				○	○
				○	○
				○	○
				○	○
				○	○
				○	○
				○	○
				○	○
				○	○
				○	○
				○	○
				○	○
				○	○
				○	○
				○	○
				○	○
				○	○
				○	○
				○	○
				○	○

Wedding Guest List

Name	Address	Phone	Invited	Gift Received	Thank you card sent
				○	○
				○	○
				○	○
				○	○
				○	○
				○	○
				○	○
				○	○
				○	○
				○	○
				○	○
				○	○
				○	○
				○	○
				○	○
				○	○
				○	○
				○	○
				○	○

Wedding Guest List

Name	Address	Phone	Invited	Gift Received	Thank you card sent
				◯	◯
				◯	◯
				◯	◯
				◯	◯
				◯	◯
				◯	◯
				◯	◯
				◯	◯
				◯	◯
				◯	◯
				◯	◯
				◯	◯
				◯	◯
				◯	◯
				◯	◯
				◯	◯
				◯	◯
				◯	◯
				◯	◯
				◯	◯
				◯	◯
				◯	◯

Wedding Guest List

Name	Address	Phone	Invited	Gift Received	Thank you card sent
				○	○
				○	○
				○	○
				○	○
				○	○
				○	○
				○	○
				○	○
				○	○
				○	○
				○	○
				○	○
				○	○
				○	○
				○	○
				○	○
				○	○
				○	○
				○	○

Wedding Guest List

Name	Address	Phone	Invited	Gift Received	Thank you card sent
				◯	◯
				◯	◯
				◯	◯
				◯	◯
				◯	◯
				◯	◯
				◯	◯
				◯	◯
				◯	◯
				◯	◯
				◯	◯
				◯	◯
				◯	◯
				◯	◯
				◯	◯
				◯	◯
				◯	◯
				◯	◯
				◯	◯
				◯	◯
				◯	◯
				◯	◯

Wedding Guest List

Name	Address	Phone	Invited	Gift Received	Thank you card sent
				◯	◯
				◯	◯
				◯	◯
				◯	◯
				◯	◯
				◯	◯
				◯	◯
				◯	◯
				◯	◯
				◯	◯
				◯	◯
				◯	◯
				◯	◯
				◯	◯
				◯	◯
				◯	◯
				◯	◯
				◯	◯
				◯	◯
				◯	◯

Wedding Guest List

Name	Address	Phone	Invited	Gift Received	Thank you card sent
				◯	◯
				◯	◯
				◯	◯
				◯	◯
				◯	◯
				◯	◯
				◯	◯
				◯	◯
				◯	◯
				◯	◯
				◯	◯
				◯	◯
				◯	◯
				◯	◯
				◯	◯
				◯	◯
				◯	◯
				◯	◯
				◯	◯
				◯	◯

Wedding Guest List

Name	Address	Phone	Invited	Gift Received	Thank you card sent
				○	○
				○	○
				○	○
				○	○
				○	○
				○	○
				○	○
				○	○
				○	○
				○	○
				○	○
				○	○
				○	○
				○	○
				○	○
				○	○
				○	○
				○	○
				○	○

Wedding Guest List

Name	Address	Phone	Invited	Gift Received	Thank you card sent
				○	○
				○	○
				○	○
				○	○
				○	○
				○	○
				○	○
				○	○
				○	○
				○	○
				○	○
				○	○
				○	○
				○	○
				○	○
				○	○
				○	○
				○	○
				○	○
				○	○
				○	○
				○	○

Wedding Guest List

Name	Address	Phone	Invited	Gift Received	Thank you card sent
				◯	◯
				◯	◯
				◯	◯
				◯	◯
				◯	◯
				◯	◯
				◯	◯
				◯	◯
				◯	◯
				◯	◯
				◯	◯
				◯	◯
				◯	◯
				◯	◯
				◯	◯
				◯	◯
				◯	◯
				◯	◯
				◯	◯
				◯	◯

Wedding Guest List

Name	Address	Phone	Invited	Gift Received	Thank you card sent
				○	○
				○	○
				○	○
				○	○
				○	○
				○	○
				○	○
				○	○
				○	○
				○	○
				○	○
				○	○
				○	○
				○	○
				○	○
				○	○
				○	○
				○	○
				○	○
				○	○

Wedding Guest List

Name	Address	Phone	Invited	Gift Received	Thank you card sent
				◯	◯
				◯	◯
				◯	◯
				◯	◯
				◯	◯
				◯	◯
				◯	◯
				◯	◯
				◯	◯
				◯	◯
				◯	◯
				◯	◯
				◯	◯
				◯	◯
				◯	◯
				◯	◯
				◯	◯
				◯	◯
				◯	◯

Wedding Guest List

Name	Address	Phone	Invited	Gift Received	Thank you card sent
				◯	◯
				◯	◯
				◯	◯
				◯	◯
				◯	◯
				◯	◯
				◯	◯
				◯	◯
				◯	◯
				◯	◯
				◯	◯
				◯	◯
				◯	◯
				◯	◯
				◯	◯
				◯	◯
				◯	◯
				◯	◯
				◯	◯
				◯	◯

Wedding Guest List

Name	Address	Phone	Invited	Gift Received	Thank you card sent
				◯	◯
				◯	◯
				◯	◯
				◯	◯
				◯	◯
				◯	◯
				◯	◯
				◯	◯
				◯	◯
				◯	◯
				◯	◯
				◯	◯
				◯	◯
				◯	◯
				◯	◯
				◯	◯
				◯	◯
				◯	◯
				◯	◯
				◯	◯

Wedding Guest List

Name	Address	Phone	Invited	Gift Received	Thank you card sent
				◯	◯
				◯	◯
				◯	◯
				◯	◯
				◯	◯
				◯	◯
				◯	◯
				◯	◯
				◯	◯
				◯	◯
				◯	◯
				◯	◯
				◯	◯
				◯	◯
				◯	◯
				◯	◯
				◯	◯
				◯	◯

Seating List

Table # or name: _____

1: _____
2: _____
3: _____
4: _____
5: _____
6: _____
7: _____
8: _____
9: _____
10: _____
11: _____
12: _____

Table # or name: _____

1: _____
2: _____
3: _____
4: _____
5: _____
6: _____
7: _____
8: _____
9: _____
10: _____
11: _____
12: _____

Table # or name: _____

1: _____
2: _____
3: _____
4: _____
5: _____
6: _____
7: _____
8: _____
9: _____
10: _____
11: _____
12: _____

Table # or name: _____

1: _____
2: _____
3: _____
4: _____
5: _____
6: _____
7: _____
8: _____
9: _____
10: _____
11: _____
12: _____

Table # or name: _____

1: _____
2: _____
3: _____
4: _____
5: _____
6: _____
7: _____
8: _____
9: _____
10: _____
11: _____
12: _____

Table # or name: _____

1: _____
2: _____
3: _____
4: _____
5: _____
6: _____
7: _____
8: _____
9: _____
10: _____
11: _____
12: _____

Seating List

Table # or name:	Table # or name:
:	1:
2:	2:
3:	3:
4:	4:
5:	5:
6:	6:
7:	7:
8:	8:
9:	9:
10:	10:
11:	11:
12:	12:

Table # or name:	Table # or name:
:	1:
2:	2:
3:	3:
4:	4:
5:	5:
6:	6:
7:	7:
8:	8:
9:	9:
10:	10:
11:	11:
12:	12:

Table # or name:	Table # or name:
1:	1:
2:	2:
3:	3:
4:	4:
5:	5:
6:	6:
7:	7:
8:	8:
9:	9:
10:	10:
11:	11:
12:	12:

Seating List

Table # or name:

1:
2:
3:
4:
5:
6:
7:
8:
9:
10:
11:
12:

Table # or name:

1:
2:
3:
4:
5:
6:
7:
8:
9:
10:
11:
12:

Table # or name:

1:
2:
3:
4:
5:
6:
7:
8:
9:
10:
11:
12:

Table # or name:

1:
2:
3:
4:
5:
6:
7:
8:
9:
10:
11:
12:

Table # or name:

1:
2:
3:
4:
5:
6:
7:
8:
9:
10:
11:
12:

Table # or name:

1:
2:
3:
4:
5:
6:
7:
8:
9:
10:
11:
12:

Seating List

Table # or name:	Table # or name:
1:	1:
2:	2:
3:	3:
4:	4:
5:	5:
6:	6:
7:	7:
8:	8:
9:	9:
10:	10:
11:	11:
12:	12:

Table # or name:	Table # or name:
1:	1:
2:	2:
3:	3:
4:	4:
5:	5:
6:	6:
7:	7:
8:	8:
9:	9:
10:	10:
11:	11:
12:	12:

Table # or name:	Table # or name:
1:	1:
2:	2:
3:	3:
4:	4:
5:	5:
6:	6:
7:	7:
8:	8:
9:	9:
10:	10:
11:	11:
12:	12:

Seating List

Table # or name:

1:
2:
3:
4:
5:
6:
7:
8:
9:
10:
11:
12:

Table # or name:

1:
2:
3:
4:
5:
6:
7:
8:
9:
10:
11:
12:

Table # or name:

1:
2:
3:
4:
5:
6:
7:
8:
9:
10:
11:
12:

Table # or name:

1:
2:
3:
4:
5:
6:
7:
8:
9:
10:
11:
12:

Table # or name:

1:
2:
3:
4:
5:
6:
7:
8:
9:
10:
11:
12:

Table # or name:

1:
2:
3:
4:
5:
6:
7:
8:
9:
10:
11:
12:

Seating List

Table # or name:	Table # or name:
1:	1:
2:	2:
3:	3:
4:	4:
5:	5:
6:	6:
7:	7:
8:	8:
9:	9:
10:	10:
11:	11:
12:	12:

Table # or name:	Table # or name:
1:	1:
2:	2:
3:	3:
4:	4:
5:	5:
6:	6:
7:	7:
8:	8:
9:	9:
10:	10:
11:	11:
12:	12:

Table # or name:	Table # or name:
1:	1:
2:	2:
3:	3:
4:	4:
5:	5:
6:	6:
7:	7:
8:	8:
9:	9:
10:	10:
11:	11:
12:	12:

Seating List

Table # or name:
1:
2:
3:
4:
5:
6:
7:
8:
9:
10:
11:
12:

Table # or name:
1:
2:
3:
4:
5:
6:
7:
8:
9:
10:
11:
12:

Table # or name:
1:
2:
3:
4:
5:
6:
7:
8:
9:
10:
11:
12:

Table # or name:
1:
2:
3:
4:
5:
6:
7:
8:
9:
10:
11:
12:

Table # or name:
1:
2:
3:
4:
5:
6:
7:
8:
9:
10:
11:
12:

Table # or name:
1:
2:
3:
4:
5:
6:
7:
8:
9:
10:
11:
12:

Seating List

Table # or name:

:
2:
3:
4:
5:
6:
7:
8:
9:
10:
11:
12:

Table # or name:

1:
2:
3:
4:
5:
6:
7:
8:
9:
10:
11:
12:

Table # or name:

:
2:
3:
4:
5:
6:
7:
8:
9:
10:
11:
12:

Table # or name:

1:
2:
3:
4:
5:
6:
7:
8:
9:
10:
11:
12:

Table # or name:

:
2:
3:
4:
5:
6:
7:
8:
9:
10:
11:
12:

Table # or name:

1:
2:
3:
4:
5:
6:
7:
8:
9:
10:
11:
12:

Seating List

Table # or name: _____

1: _____
2: _____
3: _____
4: _____
5: _____
6: _____
7: _____
8: _____
9: _____
10: _____
11: _____
12: _____

Table # or name: _____

1: _____
2: _____
3: _____
4: _____
5: _____
6: _____
7: _____
8: _____
9: _____
10: _____
11: _____
12: _____

Table # or name: _____

1: _____
2: _____
3: _____
4: _____
5: _____
6: _____
7: _____
8: _____
9: _____
10: _____
11: _____
12: _____

Table # or name: _____

1: _____
2: _____
3: _____
4: _____
5: _____
6: _____
7: _____
8: _____
9: _____
10: _____
11: _____
12: _____

Table # or name: _____

1: _____
2: _____
3: _____
4: _____
5: _____
6: _____
7: _____
8: _____
9: _____
10: _____
11: _____
12: _____

Table # or name: _____

1: _____
2: _____
3: _____
4: _____
5: _____
6: _____
7: _____
8: _____
9: _____
10: _____
11: _____
12: _____

Seating List

Table # or name:

1:

2:

3:

4:

5:

6:

7:

8:

9:

10:

11:

12:

Table # or name:

1:

2:

3:

4:

5:

6:

7:

8:

9:

10:

11:

12:

Table # or name:

1:

2:

3:

4:

5:

6:

7:

8:

9:

10:

11:

12:

Table # or name:

1:

2:

3:

4:

5:

6:

7:

8:

9:

10:

11:

12:

Table # or name:

1:

2:

3:

4:

5:

6:

7:

8:

9:

10:

11:

12:

Table # or name:

1:

2:

3:

4:

5:

6:

7:

8:

9:

10:

11:

12:

Seating Floor Plan

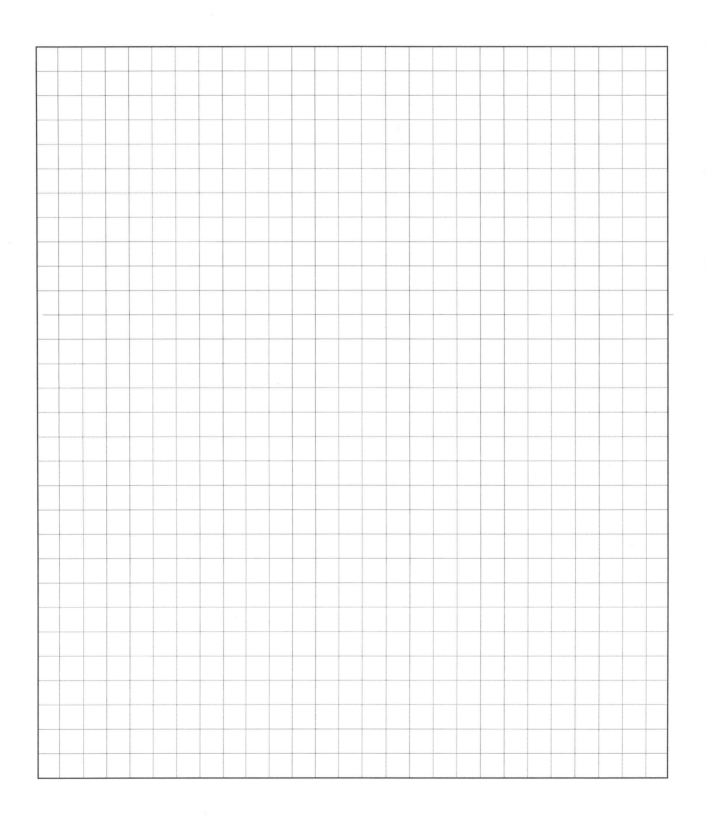

Seating Floor Plan

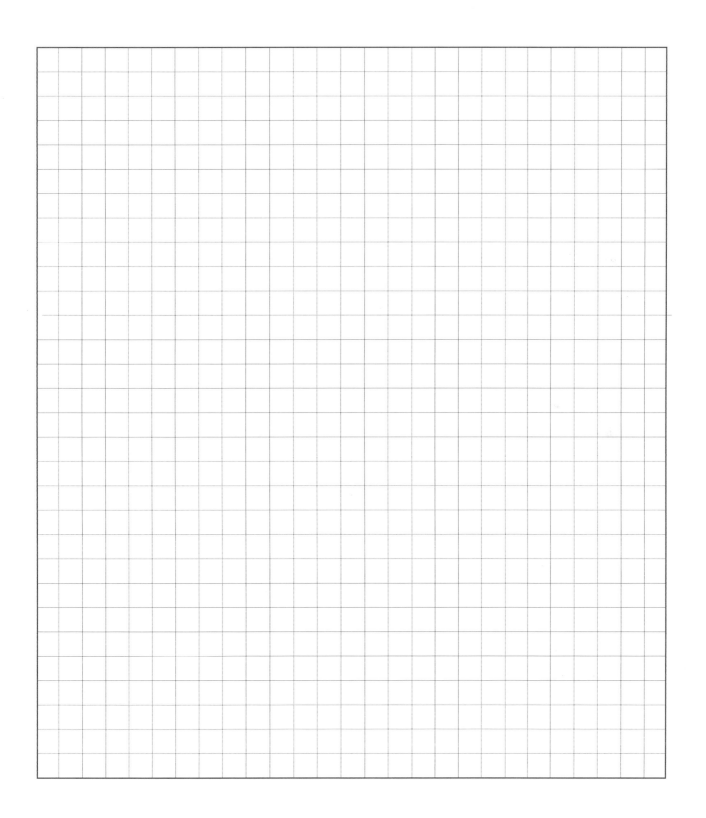

Notes

Notes

Notes

Notes

Notes

Notes

Made in the USA
Coppell, TX
11 January 2024

27529521R00072